Little Gods

Jacob Polley was born in Carlisle in 1975.
His first poetry collection, *The Brink*, published in 2003,
was a Poetry Book Society Choice and shortlisted
for the T. S. Eliot Prize.

by the same author

THE BRINK

Jacob Polley

Little Gods

PICADOR

First published 2006 by Picador
an imprint of Pan Macmillan Ltd
Pan Macmillan, 20 New Wharf Road, London N1 9RR
Basingstoke and Oxford
Associated companies throughout the world
www.panmacmillan.com

ISBN-13: 978-0-330-44420-0
ISBN-10: 0-330-44420-4

1 3 5 7 9 8 6 4 2

A CIP catalogue record for this book is available from
the British Library.

Typeset in 10 / 14.5pt Sabon
Designed by Macmillan Design Department
Printed and bound in Great Britain by
Mackays of Chatham plc, Chatham, Kent

To Sarah

Acknowledgements

Acknowledgements are due to the following:

Blinking Eye, *HQ*, *Magnetic North*, *Matter*, *Metre*, *New Welsh Review*, *Poetry*, *Poetry London*, *Poetry Review*, *The Reader*, *The Review of Contemporary Poetry*.

The author is grateful to the Author's Foundation; to Arts Council England, North East; to Arts UK; to the International Centre for the Uplands; to New Writing North; to Wendy Scott and Darlington Borough Council; and to Trinity College, Cambridge, for the Visiting Fellow Commonership in Creative Arts, 2005–07.

Particular thanks go to Imogen Cloët for her special deliveries.

Contents

Little Gods

The Owls

I hear the owls in the dark yews
behind the house – children out late
or lost, their voices worn away.
They've forgotten their names and wait

to be called again by mothers
who miss them, so they might return
with fingers and human faces.
But their sadness, too, is long gone.

Their voices are as empty
and unlovable as glass
and no one calls into the trees.

Little gods, they've forsaken us
as we have them! They sit and cry,
glorified, and couldn't care less.

You

under the dripping trees, listening to the crows'
knackered songs while the estuary glints
in the winter light. You holding your mother's purse,
the woods bare, the fields dark, and on the hill
that shocked white house where you're no longer welcome.
You setting off, the collar of your brother's coat

pulled up to your chin and the back of your neck dripped down,
wondering about London, the Thames, Dover and boats.
The hedgerows are snagged with the rain that woke you
where you lay last night in a hayloft, dreaming of rats.
You walking wet-trousered, wet-socked towards town.
You scranning Rich Teas from your rucksack.

You avoiding main roads. You warming your hands on a cow.
You on the outskirts, an industrial estate
where the kerbs are high and the corrugated sheds
hum and grind as their arc-lit interiors swing.
You in a lorry, learning Spanish with the driver
from a Teach Yourself tape. Grey miles, grey thoughts:

the rockslides caught in metal nets,
the pine forests' green domes; bare earth and bridges:
the lumpy, guileless country.
You with your fingers in the payphones' coin-trays,
palming dust from under the fruit machines.
You eating piecrusts from the plates left out

in Little Chef, watching ravens tugging bin-bags.
You in the afternoon, in the South,
in a city made of billboards and roundabouts,
looking for somewhere to ask to be dropped.
You asleep in a church porch, asleep in a graveyard,
asleep in a garden, a greenhouse, a warehouse, a wardrobe.

You washing in the yellow-tiled bogs with liquid soap,
waiting round the back of Tesco's for them to throw out the loaves.
You robbed, you running, your long fingernails.
You in the library, reading *Which?*
You on the Underground, riding all the way round,
finding the shopping list tucked in her purse:

milk potatoes broccoli cheese cheese-spread peas margarine

Black Water

There's no tin moon,
no dawn like a shaking of tambourines,
and if the clock's stopped, it's not asleep,
hasn't melted; nor did its movement march out
like a column of ants, leaving an empty case.

The knife's not a fish,
though it's cold from the drawer;
and the birch leaves aren't cymbals, though they're blown
silver-side-up in the wind, which won't show you
death in a cistern's slab of black water:
only your own untroubled face.

And there's no testing the blade of her shoulder,
there's no catch hidden in her throat,
and your heart's no more than meat.

April

Now there is only the sound of the rain
which is the shape of the streets and the ropes
of overflow knitting at the mouths of drains
and fraying from the gutters and downpipes.

Whatever the leaves were saying must wait:
rain has filled the trees with its own brisk word.
There's thunder in the darkened slates.
The pond's green eye rolls heavenwards.

You can't charge a page with the hiss, with this
cooling of the city like a new horseshoe.
Rain in the hair, at the neck and the wrists:
for rich and poor, there's rain to hurry through.

The boil and spit of pavements: mirrored brick.
Every patch of grass is fiercely lit.

Rain

as fishing nets, a wedding dress,
rain that defies rain's downwardness
and spools past the windows, frame by frame –
film after film of Edwardian rain.
Rain as a haunting, rain's ghost-train.
Rain bleeding black from the cracks in bricked-up chimneybreasts;
rain's wall-maps, rain's damp lands outlined in great stains.

Old rain, the same rain, my father's father's cold rain
taken up like a tune, confessed
to the city, hurried into the drains
and the dark and piped under playgrounds and cold-frames.
From the hills comes rain as more river, not falling
but fattening – bales of newspapers, abandoned books,
hemp ropes, rotten logs and fungi: rain feeds.

From the top bar of a five-bar gate hangs
the green world stilled in a water seed,
while the river slides by, echoing and echoey.
Rain as lost shoes; drinkers huddled like rooks.
Rain that's put paid, done you out of a day; rain's patter,
rain's slang; rain's bespittling of the spiders' webs.
Rain's pillars of smoke, rain's rooms outside the room

you watch from as rain runs through its embodiments –
a bride swinging like a bell, a lunch-hour factory crowd,
the shadow of a matchstick girl: the smudgy, underdeveloped dead
rain remembers as spaces it once rained around.
Rain's pencil-leads, rain's sketchiness,
rain writing, but whatever it tries to read back
drowned out. Rain's inconsequence to the sea.

A few pins drop then rain's loosened like hair,
or it steps with the night clean out of the air.
Rain's sound is the sound of the day undone,
the rustle of cellophane, someone and no one.
But at dawn, in the silence just after the rain,
the wet black earth of the bare field lies –
frankincense for you and I.

Spleen

after Baudelaire

When – like a lid on the mind where trouble brews –
the low sky weighs down, but leaves a chink
between earth and cloud to pour a day through
that's darker than night; when the world's a clink
with slimy walls, where Hope squeaks and flutters –
a bat among the mouldering rafters,

its wings torn and body full of dust;
when the rain's enforced, so rods of water
bar the way, restrict the view and keep us
each to our own sad cell in the Big House;
and tribes of spiders have spun their webs
in our brains, and our thoughts hatch from their eggs –

then the bells swing, suddenly furious,
and howl at the sky like homeless spirits,
and a slow cavalcade of long hearses
drives in silence through my soul, and Anguish
stands with his boot on the back of my neck
and sticks his black flag in my head.

Elder

Don't bring the hollow wood indoors
but float the flowerheads in tap-water
for two days in a stone crock, then strain
the liquor through muslin, wondering

at the time it takes a ladleful to clarify.
Sugared and stood on the cold larder floor,
one forgotten bottle blows its cork
while you lie with no ideas in the dark.

Fife

Another day forfeits its light
   to the barbarous moon
and leaves us listening to the sea

carving away with its blade of sighs.
   What might we taste tomorrow?
What might be done of all we lie

hoping in the dark to do?
   Darling, open the window.
Let the sea breathe into our room.

Greenwich

Since I'm no longer desperate for cigarettes
    I thought I could give you up in a flash
like that flash of the sun off your specs

on the day we watched cranes shift the city
    and the river's city with it.
Was I mad? Poisoned by mercury,

fluoride, or the television's oracular fumes?
    Your face is still the flame
my eyes draw on. *Must I put out my own eyes?*

Dor Beetle

Scavenger on slug flesh, shit-eater,
I wear you on my wedding finger,
your black wing-case set in a plain gold ring.

Little clock, watchman, night-singer:
your six legs tick on my skin.

At the end of love, start burrowing.

A Crow's Skull

found beside the railway line
and bleached in a tin

then sent to you
before I knew

the trouble we were in
this skull like a ring

is the least it can be
and all its candour

comes from what's lost
what's no more and is not

as mine does
now I speak of us

The Cheapjack

What do I have for as near as damn it?
What do I sell but I'm giving away?
   Might I pick my own pockets
   and slit my own throat
and dump myself dead in a shop doorway?

Daffodils, bird whistles, bobble hats,
fickle fish, slinkies, your name spelled in wire;
   caterpillars, mouse mats,
   trick plastic dog-shit,
conniptions, predictions and God's own fire.

I've bargained myself to Bedlam and back
and a wonder it is that I'm not less flesh,
   for I'd sell you the scraps,
   the loose skin, the slack,
the tips of my toes and the last of my breath

and might as well for the good my breath's done;
I've blown suits, jobs, marriages, houses and lands:
   I'm a man overcome
   by his profligate tongue
and if you get close, you can stand where I stand.

What'll it cost? Not as much as you think.
What have you got? That'll do. Here's my nod,
    here's my wink,
    here's my blood for the ink.
I'm begging you now: my life for the lot.

Accordion

My fingers on the yellow keys
and the black, the parachute strap
across my back. All I do is squeeze.

Bellows. A huge book draws breath in my lap.
I'm a strongman, bending air
till it squeals, a charmer struggling

to snap the latch on a creel of snakes.
The tattoos on my arms ache.
Behind its folds I hide my face.

Brew

I'm stewing your tea. Can't you see
my heart's steeped in it, honey?
As I wind honey round a spoon
to sweeten it, doesn't this prove
I even hold your sweet tooth dear
among all your teeth? Is it clear?
I stir in milk and the world turns
in your teacup. My stomach churns.
You warm your hands on the cup: see
how it breathes, how you throttle me?
Though the obsolete clock still ticks
I measure my time, sip by sip.
Is it hot, strong and sweet enough?
Say it's all three. Say it'll do.
Say you like something in it
but you're not sure what: I'll know.
Say when you're finished we're not
and don't go.

Telephone

I'm drinking her voice from the telephone.
I ask *Are you scrupulously alone?*
She's in company, but out on her own.
I tell her I can hear my neighbour's phone
through the wall, the man who lives on his own,
the man I would be if I stayed alone.
If she misdialled, she'd get his phone.
I tell her my house is full of her gone –
the lamps casting their lonely yellow cones,
the tortoiseshell of the telephone.
I ask *Are you glad you left me at home?*
She's glad, and shuts me back in the phone.

Mirror

I'm the mirror, half a moon above the hearth
where your faces surface then disappear:
rearrange the room and you rearrange me.
But I'm tired of looking, from wherever I'm hung
or stood, tired of never closing, tired of never turning off.
I abide by whatever's before me:
whatever's before me, I become.
Drape me in a sheet: under it I'm working.
Turn me to the wall: I pay it the closest attention.
Break me and every piece of me is full.

Beeswax

A block of beeswax, an ingot from the hive,
smelling sweeter than soap, its sweetness work's
and the perfectly-recalled honeycomb's,
cell after cell, its gold-craft riddling my mind
with light, so I have a skull not of bone,
a brain not of meat, but a wooden head
where the thought of us glows from a grid of wax.

I wait for you to lift my hackle of hair,
to pour smoke from your can of smoke
into the space behind my eyes, to reach
your bare hands in and have them gloved
with the wealth you'll bring once more to your mouth.

Dandelions

For the time we have left and the times
we've asked the time of each other,
I pack you a weightless box of fluff, blown
from the roadside dandelion clocks.
Like an arrowhead or spear-tip,
I slip in a hollow-pointed pen nib
to say winter without you will be wordless,
the water coffined and the empty trees
unmoved by the wind as it moans.
Tell me what time it is. Tell me again.
I send you all I could recover
of those frail innumerable summer moons.

The Turn

You pull the front door to
   by the cold horseshoe
for all the luck in the world has left you.

The weir shuttles sticks,
   the ignorant owl cries *who*?
You're dressed in weeds, now you've swallowed her echo,
   the moon facing you over the fields.

You drip like a cave-wall
   so hard have you swallowed,
so far down does her cold echo roll.

The night smells of matchboxes, chimneys, milk,
   rosehips, apples and river silt.
But your heart, your pinhole heart,
   cringes, blind, in its burrow.

Skin and Bone

There's not much of me left. I'm light.
I've sharpened my face. I smile like a knife.
I carry myself like the moon through the night.
If I ran now I'd run my life

out of town, against currents, tides,
all odds, good reason, fate and time,
back to her back as we lay on our sides
and I measured each breath by the length of her spine.

October, November: leaves and smoke.
The coalman pulls up in his flatbed truck.
Who would believe I stand where I am,

so long at the window, lost in a coat,
or under a streetlamp, my shadow unstuck?
Only she with her clock and her almanac can.

Twilight

Here comes the evening, the criminal's friend;
here come streetlights to kick about under,
and hedges' dark interiors to bundle loot
and bodies; here's a man calling his cat,
a door slamming, the owl's imperious hoot.

For who says work ends at day's end?
Thin girls in the dark don't. Cooks don't, cops don't.
Scribes, thieves and lovers don't. O the evening,
when wolves wear our clothes – your blazer, my business suit –
and the sky shuts us all in together!

How often have you been chased down at dusk,
cornered in your room, clawing the light switch,
while a demon scratches the back of your face
and leers from those holes where your eyes once were?

Before you can snap shut the blinds, the glass –
empty of daylight, a tablet of pitch –
throws your horror back at you! Listen.
Already the newspapers tell of tomorrow.
On the river, lanterns float. The city
lies with its throat cut and wrists open,
feeding streetlight into the water.

Ah, but the rain you prayed for. Do you hear?

Morning

The streetlamps linger on. The trees break
like waves: only you and the birds are awake.

Others lie still. Their breath comes and goes.
Under covers, facedown in their pillows,
away from the time and their minds, at peace,
elsewhere but unmoved, they sleep.

And those who've struggled for hours with the night,
men condemned to their beds, who walked or confessed,
who were caught and thrashed in sleep like a net –
even they've surrendered now, and rest.

But soon the terraces begin to smoke:
the women are up, grumbling at the sun,
and the newsagents unshutter their shops.
This is the hour of cold in the bones,
cold in the underwear, cold mirrors, old groans,
kitchens like churches, cold pews and cold stone.

Down at the quayside, the black water gropes
at the blank-faced harbour-wall, and the dreams
and the fishtails and the cabbage leaves swill
and dissolve, close to shore. A puddle steams
like a crucible, and a white boat hangs
far out and clean.

The Sun

after Baudelaire

Through the old neighbourhood, where curtains twitch
and the heat of my youth still lingers in the bricks,
while the sun hammers slate roofs and cornfields,
I practise alone with a stick for a sword.
I smell the air crackle with immanent rhymes,
kick tin cans, fall over words, bash road-signs
for the sound; translate it, then shape undreamed-of lines
to finish these poems. The sun fills our brains

and beehives with honey: he gives as a father does.
Enemy of indoor-skin, of sickness,
he burns fear from our minds, like mist from the hills,
and wakes up roses, worms, rooks and seagulls;
he shoots life into those on crutches and pills
so they skip down the backstreets like schoolgirls;
he raises crops from the earth and the heart,
laid bare before him, stirs like dark rich dirt.

When I sink with him into the city,
between chimneystacks and withered trees,
we turn fire-escapes and gutters to gold
and release the shadow from each warm stone.

Sand

To ask the cat,
the police chief and the Jezebel;
to whisper into the pink, stinking ear
    of the seashell:
where have the high tides of my talent gone?

Mother of tides, father of skies:
give me the grit to grow a pearl.
    Fill me with fear,
that brain-food, or that dark matter, desire.

    I'm flattened here,
where the ocean folds and the fierce sun
    buckles the air.
My hand sparkles idly. Might I balance
    sand-grains to build skyscrapers?

The Egg

Don't leave the clothes pegs strung out along the line,
stand up straight or you'll buckle your spine,
chew each mouthful fifty times
and talk to no one taller than our back hedge!
But a pumpkin's too heavy for me
if I have to run away from the Egg.

October's last leaves are glued to the trees
when I step outside with the front-door key.
My friends are waiting for me
with their faces made up differently,
and what's the chance there's nothing to tell
but who'll marry money or run from the Egg?

On the street there's a snuffed-out-candle smell.
Cars edge the kerbs, their headlights cast like spells
to freeze and silence us. Doorbells
and letterboxes, the broken-into shed:
suddenly I'm all alone
at the locked park gates, ready to run from the Egg.

I won't share my breath with him.
I won't share my bones.
But dad's ironing shirts, my brother stayed in,
my mum sips brown ale while the blue sirens moan.
Milk, bananas, wholemeal bread:
whatever you're made of, you can't run from the Egg.

And someone comes closer, dragging footsteps,
dragging a shadow, holding his head,
and the moon's shaken out as darkness spreads
and the whites of his eyes overflow,
and my spine's bent back so it curls my toes
and my mouth's a loosened bow
and my mouth's a loosened bow

Loss

my little sister
arriving quietly with your empty hands:
I'm afraid of you, you know me so well.

Your eyes are like mine.
If I throw you out, I'll be a witch
in my dark house with my dry heart,
turning every honest mirror to the wall.

I must have you close as I eat and sing,
your black hair flowing from your head
through my house and away

Vesta

Once I was a young girl,
searching the drawers for candles.
The world had gone out.
The night was brighter than my house.

Then I was a matchstick girl,
scratching light from the matchbox
I held under my matchstick arm,
that candle bare and cold as bone.

The wax splashed my wrist as I walked,
leading a pack of shadows down the hall.
My face trembled above my white nightgown.

Mandrake

I starved my dog Caesar and wept
to hear him whine in the small hours
of the second night. My wife slept.

By the third I could take no more,
got up, got dressed and went to him
where he lay, his head on his paws.

If it has to be done, I thought,
then let it be now. From the fridge,
fillet steak, its blood on a board,

his lead from the hook by the door.
The night had the earth on its breath.
The full moon's face hung, old and flawed.

I'd plugged my ears so all I said
I heard inside myself: *good boy*
as we walked, my sweet dog and I,

as I tied him I told him: *stay*.
He licked my hands. I backed away
and ten steps back put down that steak,

then called him to come and he came.
My teeth sang as he tore in two.
I saw the root of the earth's tongue

exposed as it screamed. My wife woke
and walked out barefoot though his blood.
She held that root. Her pale feet smoked.

That root began to hiss and kick.

English Damside

The sun rises, the sun falls.
Rats run up and down the walls.
Mushrooms grow in amber rings.
Graveyards spread their marble wings.

Children fade and screech owls wake,
their feathers smoke, their gold eyes flake.
The clocks hatch, the mirrors break:
each crack weeps a stranger's face.

Oak trees cast their leaves like light.
Blind rooms lumber through the night.
Your brother snores. Your mother shouts.

Your sleeping father walks upright.
The earth rolls on below the house.
Bowl by bowl, the fish blow out.

Caldcotes

The black trees in the small park on Caldcotes
lean out into the dusk and croon. Old crones.
They reach for the street, for those heading home:
their fingers rake windscreens; their shadows hold throats.

Through Caldcotes' trees, small voices strain.
Among Caldcotes' low branches pale faces float,
and there the flutter of red winter coats
might cause some to look, and then look again.

For who'd play on Caldcotes' steep tin slide? Who'd ride
the charred seesaw or be swung on Caldcotes'
seat and chains? Who'd heave round the roundabout,
who'd hang on, who'd seek and who'd dare to hide?

Against the wall stand uprooted headstones.
Roll over, you dead, for the little ones.

Night-doll

No witch can harm us, my dominant wife,
while rosemary grows in our garden;
and this child we find at the foot of the oak,
this child isn't ours, our monstrous issue,
nor does this night-doll mean our childlessness.
No matter the candles, in cold puddles,
the frosty tomatoes or ribbons tied
as if to hold it down; this doll, undressed
and left to sit while we slept, its glass eyes
rolled back in its plastic head, this baby
born of beetle and worm – we lift like a curse,
my dominant wife: no witch can harm us.

Votive

Day breaks the dark in two again.
The coal's cold, the log lies blackened.
The exiled owl sleeps, one eye wide.

The same sun that charges the stones,
the same light exposing the veins
    of the leaves, falls
on my head and heats up my brain:
the thoughts that grow I give to you –

Imprisoned in the rain
    the animals dig!
How we're all arranged
        like toys on tender legs!

Leaf

Vessel of water, vessel of wind;
    old yellow eye
lost in the fall, lost in the mind
    where the other leaves lie
as leaf by leaf the trees go blind.

Grass

grows on roofs, from gutters.
  The verges hunger
and nod *yes, yes, the wind is green,*
    the light's for eating;
we wear men out with our growing.

Sally Somewhere

doesn't know where:
she lifts the carpet and squints through the floor
   at dusty joists, old nails and hair;
she opens oranges and searches their quarters,
   frays her hems, unpicks her seams,
holds each dress up before a Maglite beam,
   scanning for shadows, outlines, stains.
She unscrews the U-bend and six Parker pens,
   spreads the ink out with her fingers,
explores its consistency, checks its borders,
   then finds her own hands are hidden from her.
She dislodges the cistern's white porcelain lid
   then climbs the ladder up to the attic,
where she frisks the immersion heater's red padded jacket.
   Washing-line, sink-side, bedside;
clear-sided cyclonic Dyson's insides she tries:
   nothing. She shakes each shoe,
peels each black boot from its tube of air,
   sifts flour, tests temperatures, weights;
she measures, she meters, clocks water rates,
   candle-lengths, matchstick and page numbers,
counts between lightning crack and first roll of thunder,
   then pencils the data
in diaries and maths books, on blue-gridded paper.
   She asks me. I couldn't tell her.
She kicks through leaves, looks down light-shafts; she thinks
   the flattened grass is a clue to what rested

then took off, got taken apart or rolled past
    while she slept. She's vexed; she's pestered;
won't let it arrive when it chooses, won't stop
    combing the head of the rag-haired mop
or winding the taps like the crowns of a watch.
    I say: Don't you know what you've got?

Decree

At five a.m. don't worry, sleep
and dream the un-negotiated deep
while the moon falls back to her day-blue keep
and her mercenary stars retreat.
The waking slope's too steep, too steep
to climb alone on naked feet
floorboard by cold tile by carpet by concrete
by kerbstone by iron rung to meet, to meet
whoever you must at the memorial seat
or under the sign for Eden Street
or outside the baker's, its light like heat
when you breathe on the window and write
in the mist with one finger: *wheat*.
At five are you more or less complete?
Your shadow's still held where shadows seep
when they resign our shapes and accumulate
in dismal, odourless, underground lakes;
and the face you wear is the face that fits
not the mask you assume when you wake;
and your body's no shame as it operates
softly, on standby, its sluices and gates;
and you lie where the imperial clock can't reach,
beyond all early, beyond all late –
and what might be finished, what never begun,
whatever you might claim or counterclaim,
decline, forgive, forgo or concede
must wait.

City in Winter

We're sick of the cinema,
its lobby buttered with light,
of riding home on Iron Age bikes
with smoke in our coats and our hair rock-hard,
carry-outs swinging from our handlebars.

We're waiting hopelessly for snow,
knowing it's somehow delayed by the sea
which despatches its white birds to wake us.
We ask: how long can we live at a loss,
our footsteps falling like pennies?

The city would melt us into the shops,
would draw us through blazing doorways
past scent-counters and watchcases,
our souls drab and our collars grey,
the long mirrors licking our faces.

There's a great tree in the centre
we're sick of, and our throats are wound
with inherited scarves, our heads crowned
with crap hats. Day after day,
we beg at the calendar's empty doors.

History

Here's what lasts:
the buckles and pins,

the arrowheads
but not the shafts,

piss-pots, urns and epitaphs,
false teeth; graffiti.

At Home

Old Death, in slippers and a crocheted shawl, peels
spuds at the sink or ties beans to beanpoles.

The black cloak hangs by its hood in the hall.
The famished scythe whines through the tool-shed wall.

The Byre

There's a boy in the byre after dark, after school,
with his hands on the flanks of the beasts
as they breathe. And the coffin paths and drovers' roads
and yellow-lit farmyards stand utterly still.
The running waters with their overspill,
the woods and the wetlands: all wait.

Far off, the Princes' Streets and circuses,
the bypasses and contra-flows,
the crawler lanes, carriageways, viaducts and rails
groan with their masses and traffics and freights
while delis and arcades and paper shops glow,

and the boy in the byre after dark,
after school, listens to the breathing cattle
clatter on the byre floor and knows
their heat as his, his presence as their peace
and their peace as his. The folded hills

are full of snow, the cars parked, the dogs in.
Far off, the cities grind on their axes
of orange light, while owls sweep the field's edge,
and old mines and caves of focused slate
crowd their dark around each drip as it drops.

Nothing stops, upland or low.
See who sleeps or serves, keeps or lets go,
herds or heals, builds or grows.
See the boy who brings his thoughts
to forget among the animals at nightfall –
how he leaves them quietened in the stalls.

The Prescription

Darling, d'you think you can't see as you did?
Then find inside this battered tin,
this tin that smells of cold metal and rust,
these steel-rimmed spectacles. Hook them on,
for I want you to see as you did again.
Others have. Those who've aged, or lost,
have worn them a while, and regained
lovers or sons, memories or minds,
then returned to their lives, less vague, less blind.
Now look straight at me and say what you see.
Tell me I look as I looked before,
that you feel as you felt. That I'm yours.

October

Although a tide turns in the trees
    the moon doesn't turn the leaves,
though chimneys smoke and blue concedes
    to bluer home-time dark.

Though restless leaves submerge the park
    in yellow shallows, ankle-deep,
and through each tree the moon shows, halved
    or quartered or complete,

the moon's no fruit and has no seed,
    and turns no tide of leaves on paths
that still persist but do not lead
    where they did before dark.

Although the moonstruck pond stares hard
    the moon looks elsewhere. Manholes breathe.
Each mind's a different, distant world
    this same moon will not leave.

Wild Hyacinths

Where are we, darling? The breeze
brings a blue scent. Evergreens
gather in the darkness